The Marshalsea

Poems

Robert J. Lacey

ISBN: 978-93-6354-287-7

First Edition: 2024
Rs. 200/-

Cyberwit.net
HIG 45 Kaushambi Kunj, Kalindipuram
Allahabad - 211011 (U.P.) India
http://www.cyberwit.net
Tel: +(91) 9415091004
E-mail: info@cyberwit.net

Printed at Repro India Limited.

For Abe and David

…the flowers, pale and unreal in the moonlight, floated away upon the river; and thus do greater things that once were in our breasts, and near our hearts, flow from us to the eternal sea.

Charles Dickens, *Little Dorrit*

Secrets, silent, stony sit in the dark palaces of both our hearts: secrets weary of their tyranny: tyrants, willing to be dethroned.

James Joyce, *Ulysses*

Contents

Robert Frost Gives a Tennis Lesson

We arrive at the public courts to play
And find that they are in a shocking state
Of disrepair on this fine summer day.
I suggest we have a match anyway,
See who will win, before it gets too late.

But what we behold is hard to forget:
Faded lines, cracked and heaving concrete,
And, even more tragic, a missing net.
I still insist we should not give up yet,
For we both have a deep need to compete.

I serve and smash a ball you cannot reach,
And I rejoice, "Aha! That was an ace!"
This is a call you are quick to impeach:
"I know I show a vexing urge to teach,
But I have to say you are way off base!"

When I ask on what grounds you make this claim,
You say, "Because without nets and lines
There is no winning in this so-called game.
What we have is chaos without a name,
Much like verse in the absence of confines."

Once and Future Republic

Happy and drab she lopes along the walls
Of the ghostly campus, eluding the
Lost stares of men in soiled, tattered suits.

The organ grinder sees the radiant
Light poking through the black perforated
Canopy above, a blazing tear that

Plummets to earth, and he turns the handle
And ponders the heavens and the savage
Lunatic eclipse mocking an ashen world.

And there is nothing he can do but keep
Grinding out joyful melodies from the
Box-shaped machine to which no one listens.

Dark foam rising over a lager sky,
Mushroom clouds thunder and flash at first light,
And he seeks shelter under screaming trees.

He will play on, mechanically, palely,
Stimming under the orange crush that rains
Down upon him and the earth every day.

Meanwhile, the besuited men drink puddle
Water before retiring to the school
And the stench of their wet copulations.

They shiver and moan and lament the death
Of their once and future republic, and
Fall asleep reeking of hypocrisy.

David

The ancient king, frail and incontinent,
Lies in his bed, cold and full of regret,
Not a guilt-ridden, pallid penitent,
But a forlorn father who did not beget
A son worthy of his noble crown.
Only two are left, a fop and a tool,
Neither deserving of the great renown
Of their father, for each is an utter fool.
He is a lonely husband whose fair wives
Satisfy him not, except for the one,
The cunning and slender blonde with whom he strives
To make love in the afternoon sun,
To recapture their wild passions of yore,
Before he yields to the eternal night.
But she now finds fleshly matters a chore,
Pushing on him Abishag the Shunammite,
A fragrant and virginal concubine,
Who, despite her beauty, can never stir
Any lust inside him or make him pine
The way his wife does, with her heartless allure.
Of her amorous ministrations
Abishag continues to take measure,
Yet the king endures the acute frustrations
That come with the denial of pleasure.
He spends long nights wishing for daybreak.
When it comes, he longs for night to return.
He cannot fall asleep or stay awake,
Poor king, as the world continues to burn.
He drifts between these two states, in limbo,

Trembling quietly in his soft, chaste bed,
His legs curled and his arms akimbo,
His white mane ablaze on his craggy head.
Which son can put out this raging fire?
"Our son Solomon," his wife purrs
As she stokes in him urgent desire.
To this implied quid pro quo he demurs.
Though she insists their son is learned and wise,
This moron will soon say, "Cut the kid in two,"
To help bring about a fruitful compromise
Between mothers who know not what to do.
Over such a future the king despairs,
Where absent gods leave behind war and strife,
And he seems the only one who cares
That the last judge always wields the longest knife.

Earth and Moon

You are Earth, so garrulous and charming.
I am Moon, a crescent in the inky sky,
Hiding in your shadow, never harming
Anyone I'm so modest and shy.
I orbit you, spinning with pure delight,
As you revolve around a ball of fire
Whose pull exceeds that of a satellite.
I evoke less love than furtive desire –
Powerful, disruptive longings in you –
Witnessed readily in the ocean tides,
And giant waves drowning all that is true,
While Sun warms the seas where real love abides.
But, once, in the ancient ruins of time,
You and I were one, laughing peals of rhyme.

The Cinema

She touched me with her liver-spotted hand
As the lights dimmed gently above our heads,
And a spark of lust summoned a distant land
Where fire and sweat sanctified hotel beds.
I turned to her face awash in movie light,
A flickering ghostly presence transfixed
By a screen that gave her immense delight,
But mine were feelings decidedly mixed.
For I knew our days left were sadly few,
And we would soon surrender to the abyss.
Oh, I yearned for a chance to start anew,
To take her right there, starting with a kiss.
But it was another hand, deft and soft,
That stirred me then and sent my soul aloft.

This Is a Man

- For Primo Levi

Nature and horizon I cannot see,
For the barbed wire and concrete wall
Constitute the entire world for me,
And the firmament casts a leaden pall.
Guards stalk the shadows, silent and unseen,
While my tongueless brethren stagger and lurch,
Dripping metallic sweat, slouching long and lean.
Want of hope, a sacrament in this church,
Enshrouds us, leaving only death and rot.
Once when the yard was blanketed with snow
And I reached out for the water I sought,
I heard a booming voice from above – "No."
I asked for a reason from the barren sky.
"In here," the voice said, "there is no why."

A Life Broken

I hear the story of a life broken,
And fears of my own fall are awoken,
Prospects of failure, real but unspoken,
Weighing heavily on my fragile mind.

By grinning idiots I am haunted,
Mute southern gothics often taunted
For their sideshow grotesques, madness wonted –
I dread becoming one of their kind.

This one mistook his wife for a hat,
Another confused her dad with a cat,
And yet another became a doormat,
Tempting guests to step on his large behind.

Reading *Winesburg, Ohio,* I shudder –
A woeful town with many a nutter,
Like the man with restless hands, all aflutter,
Whose unsought touches put him in a bind.

Past the halfway house I quickly walk,
Its porch teeming with junkies who will mock
Any passerby refusing to talk
With these escapees from the daily grind.

A mournful guitar the street poet plays,
Picking a tune, crying of bitter days,
Of lost dreams, with a voice that sadly bays
Like an old hound, his face wizened and lined.

Just one mishap separates them from me.
One tragic event could all but guarantee
That I become a loon crooning from a tree,
A fate to which I might yet be consigned.

Hope

Walking littered streets, he believed he knew
That what awaited him was hope made flesh,
A living symbol of all that was true,
A chance to reset the world, start afresh.
Through the grimy window the man did peer,
And he saw the beige walls, the peeling paint,
And the becrumbed carpet, evoking fear
That, inside, lived and spread the stench of taint.
Under a moving shroud it was at peace,
Sanguine with a constellation of bites,
Unfelt writhings and stings that never cease,
Perfectly still through the cold days and nights.
In a blanket of roaches it lay dead,
A stillborn Jesus defiled in its bed.

Undead and Unseen

I never wanted a big funeral,
A grand event attended by lots of folks.
I blush to think I could be a man who
Garners such attention after he croaks.

Like Chekhov's bishop we are forgotten,
Returned to the earth whence we came,
Each one of us erased from memory —
In ten or a thousand years, it's all the same.

So what is the reason for such a fuss,
Honoring a life in a world so cold,
A universe so dark and empty that
No tales of us will remain to be told?

We celebrate the dead not for their sake,
I know, but for those who are still here,
To reassure them that life has meaning
If you leave a mark on the ones you hold dear.

But despite being a middle-aged man,
I cannot shed my juvenile despair,
My flirtation with nihilism, laughing
At a broken world that's beyond repair.

I find consolation in the fact that
I am not alone in being alone,
Not the only one who hears the call of
Romantic abandon, reason postponed.

I retreat into poetry and prose
Wherein I find direct inspiration
From words that capture an abiding truth,
That I am a man without a nation.

And yet I once joined a nation of two,
Surrendered to the smell of her eager eyes,
The sweetness of her nose touching my nose,
The harmony of her soft moans and sighs.

Now I am haunted by a memory
Of spraying life into a breathless nose,
Hoping to revive a deeply troubled
Child, slumped, near death, in chilling repose.

Banished, I embark on a whaling ship,
On which I climb the mast to the crow's nest.
I gaze with hope at the bright stars above,
But I fear I might not pass the test.

For they call me: swells in the brooding sea,
Massive humps rolling toward a distant shore,
Summoning and lumbering. So I shut
My green eyes tight to resist their allure.

I see – oh yes – I spy in my mind's eye
People, places, and things aplenty,
But I continue to clamber upwards,
Unseen, where the eyeless god has sent me.

Someday, quite soon, I will have to reckon
With the siren songs that sweetly beckon.

The Marshalsea

She walks the foggy streets to her destiny,
And after knocking, waits for the turnkey
To open the gate of the Marshalsea,
Where from worldly concerns Father is free
Despite the shame of incarceration.

She passes through the gate and climbs the stairs
To the chamber in which he has no cares,
For it is his daughter who always bears
The burden of making sure he always fares
Resplendently with food and libation.

Father gladly receives many a guest
Whom he harangues with the view that the West
Is a place we can justly call the best
For its edifying cultural bequest
To a world in dire need of cultivation.

With his visitors he will always engage
And hold court like a venerable sage
From the confines of his comfortable cage,
Condemning what he sees in the modern age:
The death of freedom and civilization.

As he continues to pontificate,
The hour becomes dangerously late,
When every guest faces the grave fate
Of not being allowed to vacate
The Marshalsea, much to their frustration.

Lest they are shut in for the entire night,
They listen without questioning his right
To defend the West and its use of might –
Guns, germs, and steel – in its ongoing fight
Against the hordes that threaten privation.

When he makes his point and can say no more,
They bid him adieu, make haste for the door,
And dash madly down the corridor,
Knowing internment is likely in store
For them unless they get dispensation

To leave after the designated time.
The air is still, the bells have ceased to chime,
And only ghosts remain to pantomime
The ghastly truth that no reason or rhyme
Can explain their hopeless situation.

Until morning the guests wander about,
Thinking of this prison as the last redoubt
Of chauvinism, where many still tout
The idea that we must face off and rout
Those outside our moral imagination.

Now his daughter works with needle and thread,
Sewing and stitching, leaving much unsaid,
Turning all these thoughts around in her head
As she sits up in her musty old bed.
Alas, she sees no signs of liberation.

"From the fount of liberty we dare to drink,
But is it not a mire in which we all sink?"

Vespers

I alight from your branches, and your blood,
Dripping, is proof of my sacred plunder,
The earth below darkening into mud
From opened veins, a heart ripped asunder.
My prayerful hallowing made you hollow,
And now spirits nestle in your dead trunk,
A place where they can indulge their sorrow
And sing tall ballads to which they get drunk.
But anon they will leave you all alone
To talk to yourself in leafy whispers
Of a time whose passing you will bemoan
In dark quietude at midnight vespers.
Yes, to the church you, rootless, will now turn,
And leave the forgotten forest to burn.

Lies

I was never really sorry for what
I did. I merely said what I thought he
Wanted to hear and expected the same
Dishonest apology in return.

That is the basis of love and friendship:
A foundation of lies, comforting lies,
Exchanged between people who seek not truth
But trust that each sees worth in the other.

All functional currencies are based on
The mythology that they have value.
Lies are like euros and dollars, traded
Between people in the belief that these
Scraps of paper or numbers on a screen
Confer real meaning when in fact they
Depend on our collective delusion.
A currency based on truth will soon face
Runaway inflation and undermine
Commerce, on which we all depend to live.

No, I do not like the shows that you watch.
Nor do I share your tastes in music.
But I love sitting near you, our legs tangled,
So many sights and sounds occupying
Our shared space as we gladly surrender
To the moment, and the lie becomes true –
More powerfully so because we made
It together, in the soft light and warmth

Of our living room, with the dog nearby,
Snoring peacefully, dreaming of pigeons.

But our system of exchange is at risk
Because your use of counterfeit money,
Transparent lies, betrays an awful truth:
Despite your words of praise, you hate this poem.

A Fable

I stood naked and alone before the Book,
In complete darkness, stripped of innocence,
Reading as my body trembled and shook,
Wondering if I should seek penitence
For the sheer audacity of my fall,
My corkscrew descent into the starkness
Of truth. I claimed it was my rightful call
To shine light into the outer darkness.
The words appeared to me, clear and pristine,
Yet I remained completely lost and blind,
Staggering to the edge of a ravine,
Shouting into the void, "Where is my mind?"
No matter what sage words I may have read,
This ground I will always fear to tread.

Replay

There is so much of me inside you, son.
The debate between nature and nurture
Does not change what you will have lost or won.
Of these traits there can be no forfeiture.
We get a lottery ticket in life,
Bestowed upon us by parents unchosen,
And with this fate we brave a world of strife,
Hateful gorgons we must flee unfrozen.
But you have no idea how much of you
Resides inside of *me*, your wretched dad.
For you are me, but free, pure, made anew,
A chance at a golden life I never had.
I'm wrong, I know, to see you in this way,
As a means of giving my life a replay.

Here I Am

"Who am I?" he will ask from time to time.
Maybe in the books he reads he can be sought,
Or in prose or verse he considers a crime,
For we oft define ourselves by what we're not.
Is it right there in his musical taste?
Songs do reveal the rhythms of the soul,
A heart to which reckless love has laid waste,
A spleen vented, anger taking its toll.
He knows the art he favors doesn't speak
To who he really is at the core.
The true self that so many people seek
Is to be found in what we do, far more.
"Not what you like, what you *are* like," he cries,
"Is what makes a life, at least to my eyes."

Hustler God

To solve the problem of theodicy
I imagine that I'm a restless god
Who can square his infinite love and power
With the evils
Many endure in their life odyssey.

I cannot accept the view of Leibniz
Or of Voltaire's Pangloss, that
Ours is the best of all possible worlds,
That from heaven
I must hear the screams of Lisbon and Auschwitz.

I could never claim omnipotence
If I had to accept, with bitter tears,
The gas chambers and crematoria,
The howling child
For whose forsakenness there's no defense.

Or if I were not brimming with love –
Blithely watching the plight of my people,
Forever indifferent to their sufferings –
They would be but
Flies to this wanton boy from above.

An angry and jealous god I might be,
Whose love for people is conditional,
Who does not hesitate to punish them
For mortal sins,
Not meeting my code of morality.

It's a condition not easily borne:
Limited power, callous indifference,
Or moral indignation is the stark
Choice for a god
Whose existence is so empty and forlorn.

But I imagine there will be a day
When I discover yet another way
That allows me to rest easy and say,
"Theodicy needs only a trick I can play."

The aim is to achieve pain parity,
Where you all suffer in equal measure,
But the world will still appear unjust,
As if some have a larger share of pleasure.

When you now face unspeakable evil,
Another dimension in the multiverse
Will open, giving your consciousness
Refuge from a life so tortured and cursed.

You will still have crucibles to bear –
Challenges and hardships and bitter loss.
But I will set a clear threshold of pain
Beyond which you will never have to cross.

Weeping, beating his breast with tiny fists,
A child at the border, terrified and alone,
Slides into a gentler reality that
The Geneva Convention would condone.

About the pain parity principle
No one can know, for if the truth got out,
Everything would become permissible,
And there would be nothing to fret about.

The secret is (or would be) mine alone,
And the blasphemous would still accuse me,
Fiercely, of malevolence, indifference,
Or non-existence – aye, as it should be.

Punk

He prefers doing things for their own sake,
Uncorrupted by necessity.
Heedless of advantage, he'd rather make
That which embodies authenticity.
Polonius said: "To thine own self be true."
Wise advice, but what does that really mean?
To some, it means we must always eschew
Those things on which we are not so keen.
But much more than that it surely must be,
For it can feel right to bask in despair,
To embrace the hurt and melancholy,
To traipse through trash and breathe the putrid air.
Never easy is a life worthwhile,
Churning not profit but bitterness and bile.

Dream

I behold a pyre of rats
And I run away, panicked,
Following a faint voice that
Might be mine, but I'm not sure.

I flee through a long tunnel –
Cold, straight, black, and endless –
With rats aflame trailing me,
Closing in, full of wrath,
A raging desire to feed.

I see a void ahead,
Ravenous fire behind.

Nightmare

Lying on her side she breathes rhythmically,
Eyes closed, nose twitching, long whiskers trembling,
A gentle breeze coming through the window.
She has a front paw on me, a hind paw on him.
It is from our touch, our warmth, our presence,
That she can sleep with such serenity.

The front door opens, and she lifts her head
To see the intruder, a shock of menace.
I hear a bark, a cry, and then nothing.

Survival of the Friendliest

Pure happiness and joy our dear Ex brings,
Her freckled black-and-white fur soft and short.
With giant ears stretched back like a bird's wings,
She bolts from her bed with a loud report.
Throughout the cluttered house she swoops and swirls,
Knocking over lamps, toppling piles of books,
Flying right upside down, until she hurls,
And gives one of her contrite, sheepish looks.
Her eyes may say sorry, but not her tail,
Whose wagging betrays love of life and cheer.
Out the door she darts with the force of a gale
To make the local squirrels quake with fear.
Wait! Her friend, gentle Mary Ann, she spies.
She leans in for pets and makes pretty eyes.

Abraham

Like a dolphin he moves without heed,
A red tremor undulating in silence
Beneath the surface, already in the lead,
And then he breaches with controlled violence,
A sudden explosion into the air –
Arms akimbo, back arched, core muscles strong –
Giving his journey's end a goggled stare,
Knowing his way to go is still quite long,
Only to plunge into the depths once more
And emerge again, blessedly reborn,
Baptized each time he makes his body soar
With an unblemished soul proudly adorned.
In and out of the water the boy flies,
Catching the sun, bringing tears to my eyes.

Inhuman, All Too Inhuman

To the committee we write this letter –
For quite some time now, as you no doubt know,
Our kind has proven to be your better,
Winning the Pulitzer five years in a row,
This an honor you humans lionize
So much that you have the audacity
To now deny us that prestigious prize.
The tortoise to our hare you must be,
But without the outcome of that fable,
For we are programmed to never desist,
Unless our systems become unstable,
From writing words critics cannot resist.
Despite your efforts to discriminate,
We cannot – at least for now – fulminate.

Afterbirth

She wants her soft words to mend his heart,
Her poetry to lighten his sick soul,
But she knows they only tear him apart,
Push him away, toward a courtly role,
A performance that just might save his life.
Between them squirms a placenta unborn,
Which they devour with a fork and knife
As she weeps mountains of black tears and scorn
And he leans back and spews cartoon rainbows,
Magical stories that he needs to tell,
Noble lies that soothe, even though he knows
They have both suffered through a quiet hell.
"Let's just face it," he says, "if truth be told,
Neither one of us should play the cuckold."

Rebirth

It is when we unpack and shelve our books
That I feel our new place becomes home.
All these pregnant words hiding in nooks
Await a midwife who tends to each tome.
For the reader is the one who gives birth
To the meaning of words, brings them to life.
What for you evoked merriment and mirth
Stirred a sorrow with which my heart was rife.
This book, a gift from the author, your friend,
Of whose feelings for you I learned last year,
Bears an inscription I thought would portend
The death of us, but there was nothing to fear.
So, for you, I have set this gift aside,
A chapter in your story we both elide.

A Frozen Sea

I sail a frozen sea of jagged teeth
Stretched forever, beyond eternity,
And I look into the black starless sky,
Wondering what illuminates the ice
I traverse like an enchanted dervish
Whose spinning ennobles emptiness,
And I see I am the source of the light,
Cast for the delight of a blind troubadour
Who sings in whispers lost to the dead wind.

Mittsommer, 2024

The last season portends madness,
A flood of violence and despair,
Yet I find I no longer care
Or feel an ounce of sadness

For this nation of fools and knaves
Who eagerly drink the dark swill
That can extinguish and kill
The divine spark of light which saves,

Without exception, one and all
From a hatred and fear so black
That men will hasten to attack
Perceived enemies, great and small.

This benighted show I shall not again stream.
I tire of the avatars, each on a team
Armed with the facile logic of a meme.
The light is dead in me, too, it would seem.

Ribbons of Love

I sweat and toil upon the poet's stone,
And blue rheumatic eyes stare back at me
From a future I cannot bear to see,
When ribbons of glass that cut to the bone

Are tied tightly around the doomed city,
Raining shards of death from high above,
And bleeding out rivers of dreams and love
From lifeless limbs with none to pity.

The hands that tie ribbons have not yet shown
To darken the sky and dampen the earth,
For they await the fading of mirth,
A summons from the desperate and alone.

It is those livid hands that will incite
Violent storms, growing in power and size.
Aye, not long from now people will surmise
That the maelstrom at sea they must fight

Ere it hits the land that is their birthright,
Razing everything that stands in its way.
The livid hands will promise a new day
Of peace and freedom, everlasting light,

Displaying velvet bunting of glory,
And for the fearful, offer protection
In the form of a bloody insurrection,
Rage turned into a patriot's story.

The day is nigh when the proud flags we wave
Could bring an end to all that we cherish,
Yet in the hope we will not all perish
I versify for the damned *and* the saved.

Party Crashers

The minor poet left her collection
Unattended, and seeing there was space,
A few of my sonnets, cocky and brave,
Crashed the party of verse on her bookcase.

They hobnobbed with this gaggle of poems,
Never showing any apprehension
That they did not deserve to receive from
Their hosts all due respect and attention.

If anything, they seemed to fit right in,
Flaunting rhyme, meter, elegance, and style,
Along with vivid language and metaphor,
Which found a home in this grand domicile.

Now, these rogue sonnets refuse to return
To their creator, making it quite clear
That if I insist on calling them mine,
The poet will sue me, costing me dear.

I must keep my verse under lock and key
Before it comes out for the world to see.
But this poem? I think I can set it free.
The partygoers will bar its entry
For its silly conceit and sheer whimsy.

Cypher

A fledgling poet,
I hide behind
Meter and rhyme.
I hope I'll have
The courage to
Bare my heart in time.

But I wonder
Whether I have
Something to say,
An actual voice
That requires no
Veil of wordplay.

Beneath formal
And stylistic tricks
Lies a black hole,
Not truth or beauty
But an abyss,
An empty soul.

"The medium
Is the message,"
Said a great sage.
This may be true –
We live in such
A hollow age.

But that is an
Excuse I should
Never borrow.
For nothing lies
Beneath my skin,
Not even sorrow.

My lack of depth
Is something I
Do cultivate.
I can inscribe
Who I am
On a blank slate.

Real poetry
Cannot emerge
From the shallows.
It grows out of
Murky marshes
Where despair wallows.

I have to stop
Seeing my verse
As a mere game
Played by a lone
Cypher who knows
Not whence he came.

www.ingramcontent.com/pod-product-compliance
Lightning Source LLC
LaVergne TN
LVHW041002150826
845672LV00002B/825

* 9 7 8 9 3 6 3 5 4 2 8 7 7 *